SILVER BURDETT & GINN
SOCIAL STUDIES

Communities and Their Needs

BOBBIE P. HYDER
Elementary Education Coordinator
Madison County School System, Huntsville, Alabama

MARY GARCIA METZGER
Dean of Instruction
Dowling Middle School, Houston, Texas

SILVER BURDETT & GINN

MORRISTOWN, NJ • NEEDHAM, MA
Atlanta, GA • Cincinnati, OH • Dallas, TX • Menlo Park, CA • Deerfield, IL

SERIES AUTHORS

Val E. Arnsdorf, Former Professor, College of Education, University of Delaware, Newark, Delaware

Herbert J. Bass, Professor of History, Temple University, Philadelphia, Pennsylvania

Richard C. Brown, Former Professor of History, State University of New York College at Buffalo

Patricia T. Caro, Assistant Professor of Geography, University of Oregon, Eugene, Oregon

Kenneth S. Cooper, Professor of History, Emeritus, George Peabody College for Teachers, Vanderbilt University, Nashville, Tennessee

Gary S. Elbow, Professor of Geography, Texas Tech University, Lubbock, Texas

Alvis T. Harthern, Professor of Early Childhood Education, West Georgia College, Carrollton, Georgia

Timothy M. Helmus, Social Studies Instructor, City Middle and High School, Grand Rapids, Michigan

Bobbie P. Hyder, Elementary Education Coordinator, Madison County School System, Huntsville, Alabama

Theodore Kaltsounis, Professor and Associate Dean, College of Education, University of Washington, Seattle, Washington

Richard H. Loftin, Former Director of Curriculum and Staff Development, Aldine Independent School District, Houston, Texas

Mary Garcia Metzger, Dean of Instruction, Dowling Middle School, Houston, Texas

Clyde P. Patton, Professor of Geography, University of Oregon, Eugene, Oregon

Norman J.G. Pounds, Former University Professor of Geography, Indiana University, Bloomington, Indiana

Arlene C. Rengert, Associate Professor of Geography, West Chester University, West Chester, Pennsylvania

Robert N. Saveland, Professor of Social Science Education, University of Georgia, Athens, Georgia

Edgar A. Toppin, Professor of History and Dean of the Graduate School, Virginia State University, Petersburg, Virginia

GRADE-LEVEL CONTRIBUTORS

Lorraine Cooley, Teacher, Nathaniel Hawthorne School, Rochester, New York

Russell Erickson, Teacher, Zachery Lane School, Minneapolis, Minnesota

Katherine V. Kalmbach, Teacher, J. W. York School, Raleigh, North Carolina

Rita Nerz, Teacher, Perry School, Erie, Pennsylvania

Eleonor Nicolls, Teacher, Clendenin School, El Paso, Texas

Mary Louise Trujillo, Teacher, Talta School, Ranchos de Taos, New Mexico

CONTENTS

Maps

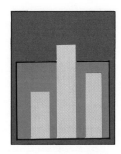

Using Skills

Learning About Communities

community

neighborhood

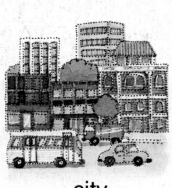

city

apartment
building

factory

museum

suburb

town

What is a community?

Most people like to live near other people.
A **community** is a place where people live.

In some communities there are many
neighborhoods.
A neighborhood is a part of a community.
The people in a neighborhood are neighbors.
Neighbors sometimes help each other.

AMITY ELEMENTARY SCHOOL

Communities are alike in many ways.
They all have homes, stores, and schools.
There are buildings where people work.
There are places where people have fun.

What is a city?

A **city** is a large community where
many people live and work.
Often, people in cities live in **apartment buildings**.
An apartment building is a home for many families.

People work at many kinds of jobs in a city.
They work in office buildings, stores, and
factories.
A factory is a place where things are made.
This factory worker is making toy cars.

All cities have places where people have fun.
These people are enjoying a baseball game.

There are parks in most cities.
People in this park are
putting on a circus show.
There is plenty of space for
other people to sit and watch.

There is a zoo in most large cities.
Animals are fun to watch.
Some animals are fun to ride.

Most cities have at least
one **museum**.
A museum is a building
where different groups
of things are shown.
Every museum has many
interesting things to see.
Museums help us learn
how people lived long ago.
They give us ideas about
what the future may be like.

What is a suburb?

Most large cities have communities all around them.
A community just outside a city is called a **suburb**.
Suburbs are usually smaller than cities.
They are often less crowded.
In suburbs most homes are for one family.

Children in suburbs do many
of the things that city children do.
They ride bicycles.
They play a ball game called soccer.
They have fun on a slide.
What kinds of things do you enjoy
in your community?

11

People who live in a suburb often work
in a nearby city.
They travel between the suburb and the city
every work day.
Some people go to work by train or by bus.

Some drive their car to work.
Some share a ride with other people.

Suburbs also have places where people work.
These people work in an office building
in a suburb.
The office building is much smaller than most
office buildings in a city.
Notice the trees and grass near the building.

What is a farm community?

A farm community has fewer people than a city or a suburb.
A farm community has a lot of land and open spaces.
Most people live and work on their farms. They often grow vegetables, such as corn and potatoes.
On some farms, animals are raised for food.
Most of our food comes from farm communities.

Many farm communities are
near **towns**.
A town is a small community.
It is much smaller than a suburb.
In this town there is only one
main street.
All the stores in the town are
on that street.

There are many jobs to do on a farm.
Young animals need special attention.
Chickens have to be fed and given fresh water.
Fields have to be planted and cared for.

Machines help to do some of the work on a farm.
Farm children also help with the work.
Some children help care for the farm animals.
Farm animals need care every day.

Sometimes friends come together to get a job done.
Picking pumpkins can be more fun than work when everyone helps.

Identifying the Seasons

In many communities the weather changes
during the year.
The changes in weather make four seasons.
The four seasons are spring, summer, fall,
and winter.

The pictures on page 19 show the four seasons.
Look carefully at the pictures.

Read the following sentences.
Name the season that each sentence describes.
Write your answer on a sheet of paper.
Number your paper from **1** to **4**.

1. Many plants and flowers begin to bloom.
2. The leaves on some trees turn red, yellow,
and orange.
3. There are many hot days.
4. Homes in most communities have to be heated.

Spring

Summer

Fall

Winter

Unit 1 Review

Main Ideas

1. A community is a place where people live.

2. A neighborhood is a part of a community.

3. A city is a large community.

4. A suburb is a community near a large city.

5. A farm community has fewer people than cities and suburbs have.

Vocabulary Review

Number your paper from **1** to **4**.
Write the word that matches each picture.

city

suburb

museum

factory

Unit Checkup

1. What is a community?
2. What is a large community called?
3. What is a community near a city called?
4. How are cities and suburbs alike?
5. Why do farm communities need a lot of land?

Applying Knowledge

1. Pretend you have a new neighbor.
You want your neighbor to learn about your community.
Draw pictures of important places in your community.
2. Find a picture of any kind of a community.
Tell what kind of community it is.

Learning About Maps

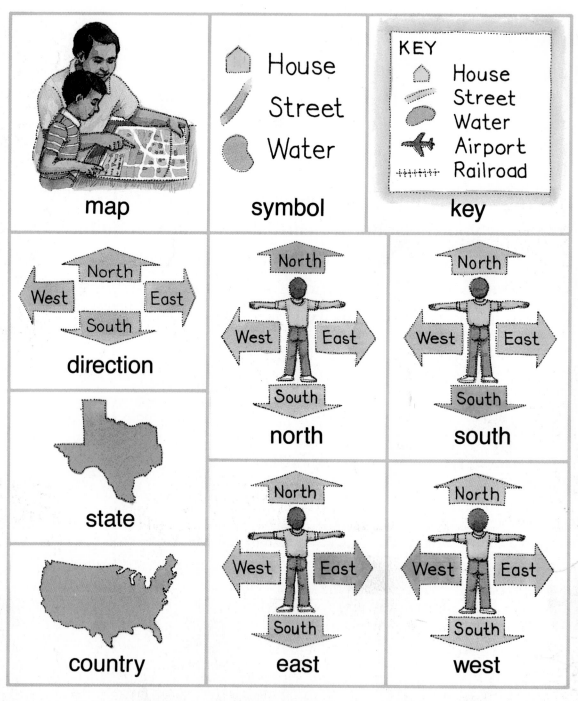

map

symbol

KEY

House
Street
Water
Airport
Railroad

key

direction

north

south

state

east

west

country

What is a map?

A community has many places for having fun.
A park is one place for sharing good times.

On page 25 there is a **map** of a park.
A map is a special kind of picture.
A map shows the earth or part of the earth.

Every map has **symbols.**
Symbols stand for real things and real places.
Every map has a **key.**
The group of pictures below the map is the key.
The key tells what real things and places
the symbols stand for.

KEY

 SWIMMING POOL

 MERRY-GO ROUND

 STAIRS

 TREES

 FOOD STAND

 WATER

 GRASS

 PATHS

 BENCHES

 BRIDGE

 FLOWER BEDS

How is a map like a picture?

The picture on this page shows part
of a community.
It was taken from an airplane.
It shows how the community looks from the air.
The map on page 27 shows the same places
the picture shows.

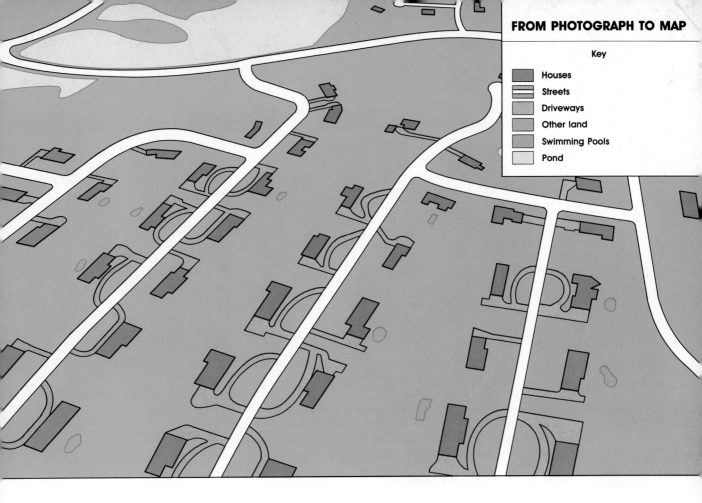

In some ways the picture and the map are alike.
In other ways they are different.

   Look at the key for this map.
Find the symbol for the pond.
Find the pond on the map.
Find the pond in the picture on page 26.

How do directions help us?

Let's look at another picture.

There are many things to see in this picture.

Find the bridge.

An airplane is flying <u>over</u> the bridge.

There is a road <u>under</u> the bridge.

Two workers are directing traffic on the bridge.

One worker is holding a flag <u>up</u>.

Another worker is holding a flag <u>down</u>.

Notice the worker at the <u>bottom</u> of the picture.

He is holding a flag in his <u>left</u> hand.

28

Find the worker near the <u>top</u> of the picture.
She is holding her flag in her <u>right</u> hand.

  Some of the words on these pages have
a line under them.
These are all **direction** words.
A direction word tells where something is.
<u>Over</u> and <u>under</u> and <u>up</u> and <u>down</u> are direction words.
<u>Top</u> and <u>bottom</u> and <u>left</u> and <u>right</u> are
also direction words.

What special directions do maps have?

All maps have four important directions.
They are **north, south, east,** and **west.**
North and south are opposite each other.
So are east and west.

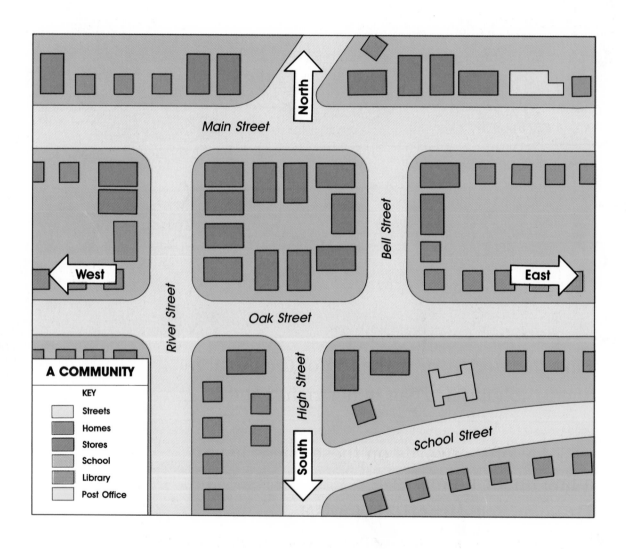

East is the direction from which the sun seems
to rise every morning.
The sun seems to set toward the west.
When you face north, east is always to your right.
When you face north, west is always to your left.
North, south, east, and west help you know
where you are.

Which is larger, a city or a state?

Your community is part of a **state.**
There are many communities in a state.
Some communities in a state are cities.
A state is much larger than a city.

The city in this picture is Columbus.
It is in the state of Ohio.

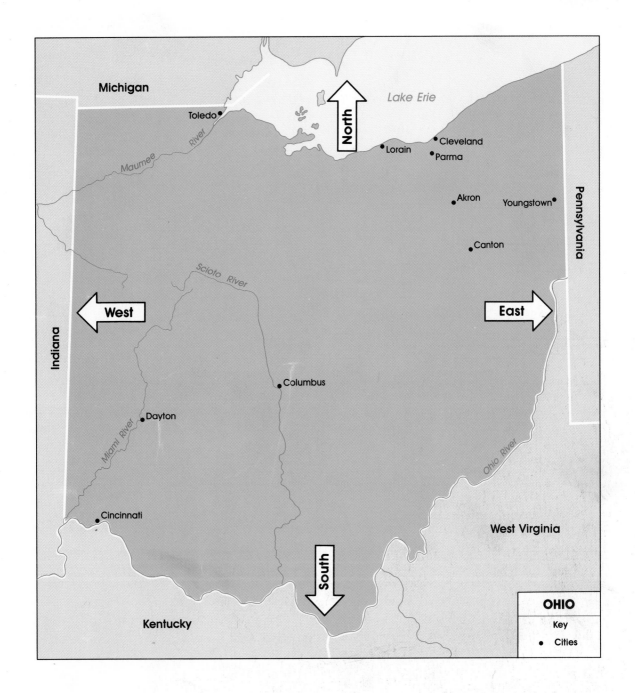

Look at the map.

It shows the state of Ohio.

The names of some cities in Ohio are on the map.

Look at the map key.

Find the symbol for cities on the map.

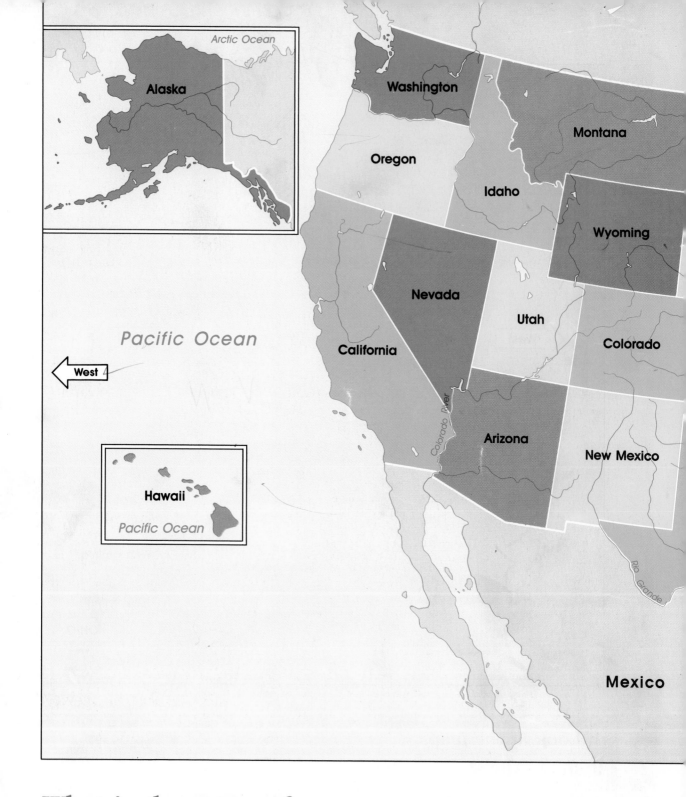

What is the name of our country?

We live in the United States of America.
The United States of America is our **country.**

This is a map of the United States of America.

There are 50 states in our country.

Each state in the United States has a name.

How is each state in the United States special?

There are some special things about each state
in the United States.
Each state has a name.
Each state has its own special flag.
Look at these state flags.
How are they alike?
How are they different?

North Carolina

Hawaii

California

Washington

Illinois

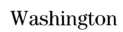

Oklahoma

Using Map Directions

Directions help us in many ways.
They help us know which way to go.
They help us find places on a map.

The map on page 39 shows a zoo.
Pretend that you are at the Zoo Entrance.
Use the map to answer these questions.
Write the answers on a separate sheet of paper.

1. Is the Parking Area north or south
of the Pony Rides?
2. Is the World of Birds north or south
of the Gift Shop?
3. Is the Seal Show north or south
of the Pony Rides?
4. Is the Gift Shop east or west of the Entrance?
5. Is the Elephant House east or west
of the World of Birds?
6. Is the Seal Show east or west of the Monkeys?

Unit 2 Review

Main Ideas

1. A map is a drawing of the earth or part of the earth.
2. Every map has symbols and a key.
3. A direction word tells where something is.
4. All maps have four important directions. They are north, south, east, and west.
5. A state is much larger than a city.
6. The United States of America is our country.
7. Each state in the United States has a name.
8. Each state in the United States has a special flag.

Vocabulary Review

Number your paper from **1** to **6**.
Choose the right word for each sentence.

east   direction   state
key   country   symbols

1. Every map has a _____.
2. In every map key there are _____.
3. North is a _____.
4. The sun seems to rise in the _____.
5. A city is smaller than a _____.
6. The United States of America is our _____.

Unit Checkup

1. What do symbols on a map stand for?

2. Why does a map have a key?

3. What four direction words help people read a map?

4. If you know which way north is, how can you find east?

5. How many states are there in the United States?

Applying Knowledge

1. Make a map of your bedroom.
Draw symbols to show the different things
in the room. Make a key for the map.

2. Make a list of some of the things you like
about your state.

3. Look at a map of the United States of America.
Make a list of things the map shows about
our country.

Learning About the Earth

continent	ocean	globe	model
plain	mountain		river
lake	island		peninsula

43

What is a continent?

The United States of America is part
of a **continent**.
A continent is a very large body of land.
The map on page 45 shows the continent
of North America.
We live on the continent of North America.

Find the United States of America on the map.
Canada and Mexico are also on the continent
of North America.
Canada is north of the United States.
Mexico is south of the United States.
Canada and Mexico are our nearest neighbors.

Alaska
(U.S.)

North

Canada

Pacific
Ocean

West

United States of America

East

Atlantic
Ocean

Mexico

NORTH AMERICA

South

45

This is a map of the whole earth.

It shows all the continents.

There are seven continents.

Each continent has a name.

Which continent is farthest away from our continent?

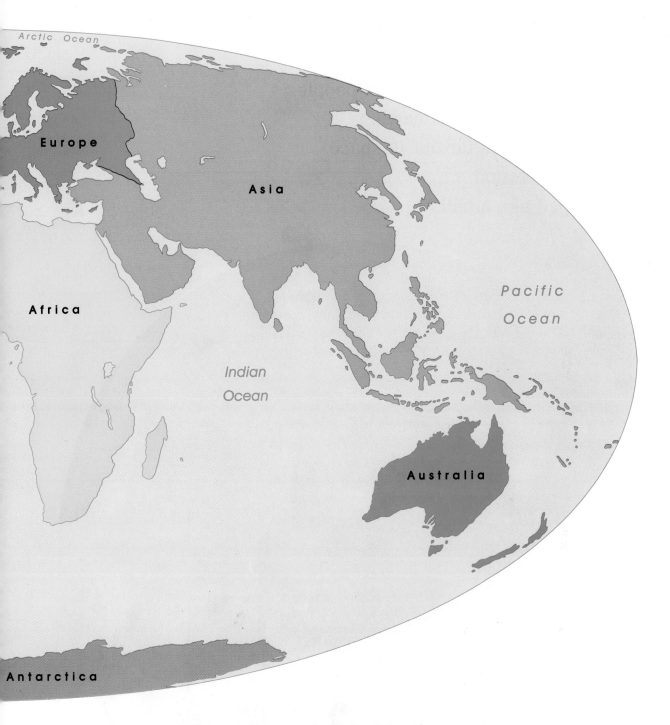

This map also shows the earth's **oceans**.

An ocean is a large body of water.

There are four oceans on the earth.

Each ocean has a name.

Which oceans touch the continent of North America?

What is a globe?

The earth is the home of all people.
Here is a picture of the earth.
It was taken from far out in space.
The earth is round.
It is shaped like a ball.

The picture on this page shows a **globe.**

A globe is a **model** of the earth.

A globe shows the land on the earth.

It shows the water, too.

Earlier you learned that all maps have at least four special directions. Two of the directions are north and south. The globe helps us see where north and south are. North is the direction toward the North Pole. The North Pole is the most northern place on the earth. The North Pole is a real place! The boy is pointing to the North Pole on the globe.

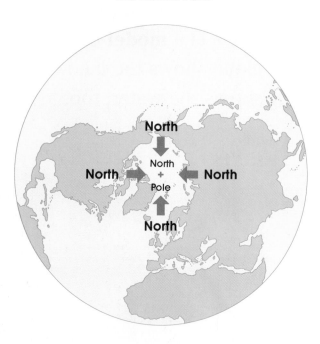

56

South is the direction toward the South Pole. The South Pole is another special place. It, too, is a real place. The South Pole is the most southern place on the earth. The boy is pointing to the South Pole on the globe. The South Pole is opposite the North Pole.

THE SOUTH POLE

Where do people live?

People live in many different places.
Some people live where the land is flat.
Land that is flat is called a **plain**.
Most plains are good for farming.

Some people live in communities near **mountains**.
A mountain is very high land.
It rises above the land around it.
Mount McKinley is the highest mountain in our country.
It is in Alaska.

Some communities are near **rivers.**
A river is a long body of water
that flows through the land.
The river in this picture is the
Hudson River.
The Hudson River is in New York.
It is deep enough for large ships
to travel on its water.

Some people live near **lakes**.
A lake is a body of water with land all around it.
A lake is much smaller than an ocean.

There are communities on
or near **islands**.
An island is land with water
all around it.
One of our states is made
up of islands.
It is called Hawaii.
Find Hawaii on the map
on pages 34 and 35.

The community in this picture is on a **peninsula.**
A peninsula is land that has water nearly all the
way around it.

Most of one state in the United States is a peninsula.
It is the state of Florida.

Find Florida on the map on pages 34 and 35.

Naming Parts of the Earth

The drawing above shows different parts
of the earth.
Look carefully at the drawing.
Then answer the questions on page 57.
Write the numbers **1** to **6** on a sheet of paper.

1. Is <u>A</u> a lake or an island?
2. Is <u>B</u> an island or a peninsula?
3. Is <u>C</u> a peninsula or a mountain?
4. Is <u>D</u> a lake or a river?
5. Is <u>E</u> a plain or a mountain?
6. Is <u>F</u> a plain or a peninsula?

Unit 3 Review

Main Ideas

1. A continent is a very large body of land.
2. A globe is a model of the earth.
3. North and south are two important directions.
4. Land that is flat is called a plain.
5. A mountain is very high land.
6. A river is a long body of water that flows through the land.
7. A lake is a body of water with land all around it.
8. An island is land with water all around it.
9. A peninsula is land that has water nearly all around it.

Vocabulary Review

Number your paper from **1** to **6**.
Choose the right word for each sentence.

ocean	mountain	island
plain	peninsula	continent

1. North America is a _____.
2. Atlantic is the name of an _____.
3. Very high land is called a _____.
4. Flat land is called a _____.
5. Land with water all around it is called an _____.
6. Land with water nearly all around it is called a _____.

Unit Checkup

1. On which continent is the United States?

2. Which two countries are the nearest neighbors of the United States?

3. What does a globe show about the earth?

4. Why are most plains good for farming?

5. How is a peninsula different from an island?

Applying Knowledge

1. Look at a globe in your classroom. List what you can learn about the earth by looking at the globe.

2. Look at a map of the United States. Point to a large lake. Find a long river. Find an island. Find a peninsula.

Learning About Needs and Wants

needs

wants

income

budget

savings

taxes

products

services

Cold Lemonade
10cents

What are needs?

All people have **needs**.
Needs are things people must have to live.
There are certain things that people cannot
do without.
Everyone must have food to eat.

People need clothes to wear.

62

People need shelter.

Food, clothes, and shelter are basic needs.
All people need these three things.
The three basic needs are the same for everyone
wherever they live.

What other needs do people have?

Think of someone you love very much.
Think of someone who loves you.
How do you feel when that person hugs you?
Love is a very important need.
People everywhere need love.

64

Food, clothes, and shelter
are basic needs.
But people need more than
these things.
Imagine a world without friends.
Imagine a world without fun.
People need love and friends.
They need to have fun.

What are wants?

All people have **wants**.
Wants are things people would like
to have but can do without.
Pets and games and toys are wants.

A vacation is a want.

People can live without the things they want.
But wants are important, too.
Wants help make life enjoyable.

What is income?

Many things that people need and want
cost money.
People work to earn money.
This woman is working as a photographer.
She takes pictures.
The money she earns for her work
is called **income**.

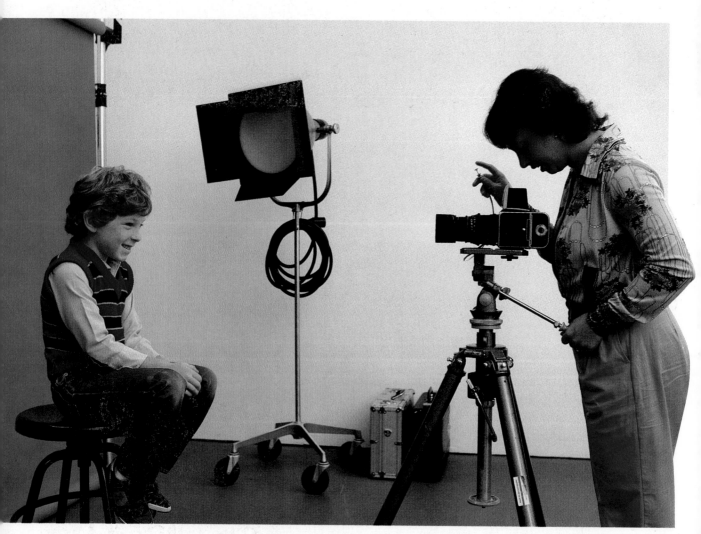

She wants to use her income wisely.
She and her husband agree on a budget.
A **budget** is a spending plan.
It helps people know how much money
they can spend on needs and wants.

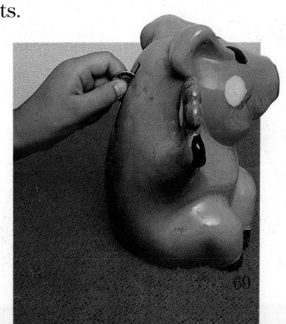

Savings are an important part
of a budget.

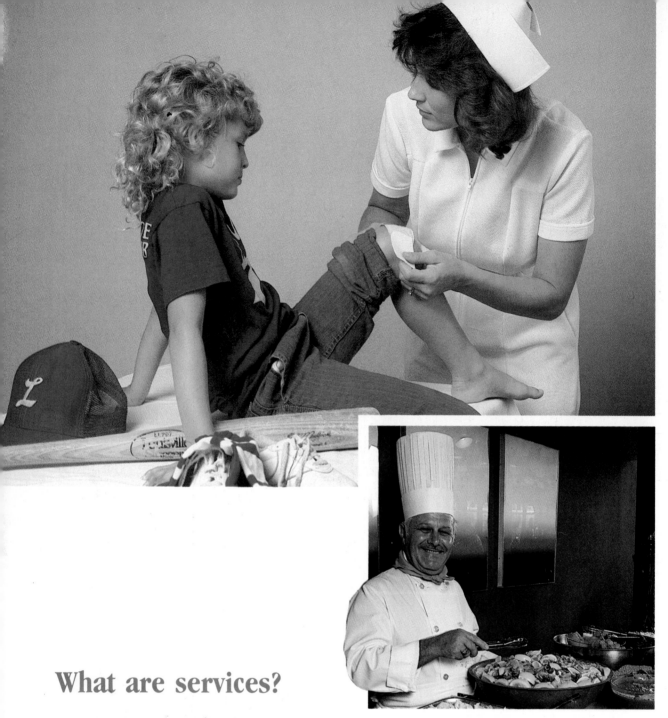

What are services?

There are many different kinds of workers.
Some workers do things for other people.
These workers provide, or give, **services**.
A service is a kind of work that helps people.
Taking care of someone who is hurt is a service.
Serving food in a restaurant is a service.

70

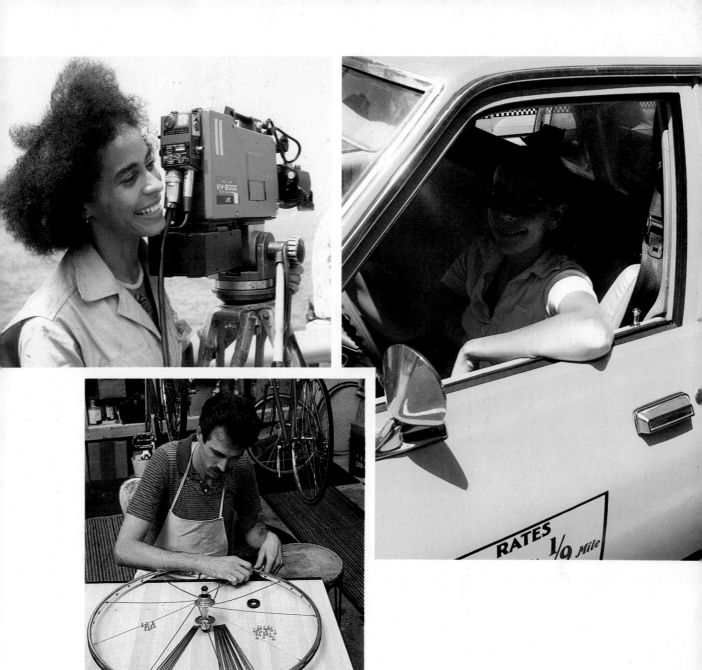

People who provide a service are called
service workers.

The people shown in these pictures are
service workers.

What services are they providing?

Some service workers work for the
community.
Their work helps everyone in the community.
Fire fighters and police officers are
community service workers.
So are people who remove snow
from community streets.

A librarian is also a community service worker.
A community depends on its service workers.

The people who live in the community pay money
for the service of these workers.
That money is called **taxes**.

The community pays its service workers
with the money from taxes.
Community service workers earn their income
from the community.

What are products?

Not all workers provide services.
There are workers who grow the food we eat.
There are workers who make the things we use.
The things workers grow or make are called **products**.

A map puzzle is also a product.
Let's look at how a map puzzle is made.
First a flat board is painted white.
A large roller is used to spread the paint evenly.
The shape of all the states in the United States
is then printed on the white board.

A machine is used to cut out each state.

The machine is called a jigsaw.

This worker is cutting out the outline of the map.

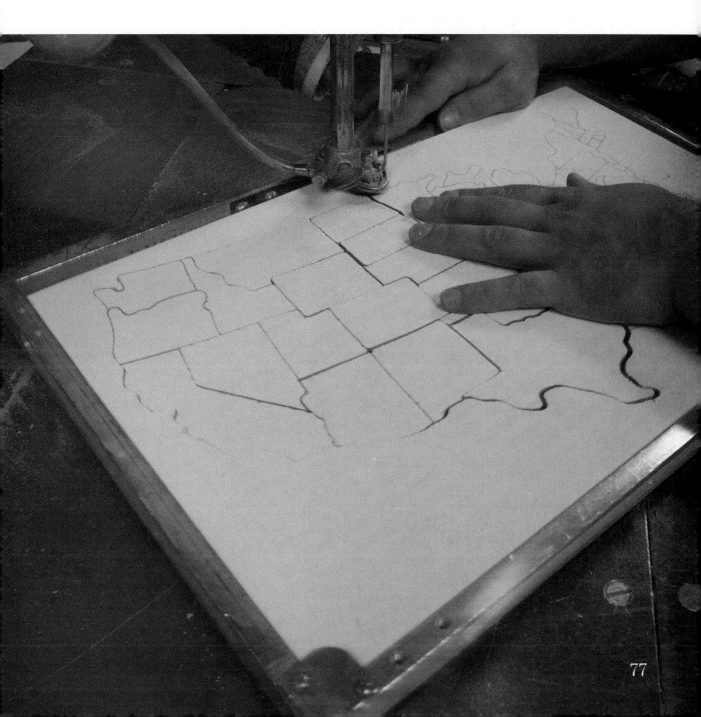

The states are separated
into several groups.
A worker then puts each group
of states into flat baskets.
All the states in a basket will be
painted with the same color.

The states are now ready
to be painted.
A worker sprays paint
on the states.
Some states are painted blue.
Some are painted yellow.
Other states are painted either
green or pink.

The baskets of states are sent
to another worker.
He puts the states where they belong
in the puzzle of the United States.

Another worker prints the name of the map
on the puzzle.
She also prints the names of the states
on the map.
Black ink is used to print the names.

Finally the map is finished.
It is then wrapped in plastic.
The plastic keeps the pieces
of the puzzle in place.

Twelve map puzzles are put into a box.
The boxes of puzzles are sent all over
our country to be sold.

80

Now children everywhere can have fun
learning about our states.

Reading a Picture Graph

Mrs. Carter owns a store.
In her store she sells toys and games.
She also sells kites.

Look at the drawing on page 83.
It shows how many kites Mrs. Carter sold
in one week.
This drawing is called a picture graph.

Study the picture graph.
Then answer these questions.
Write your answers on a separate sheet of paper.

1. How many kites were sold on Monday?

2. How many kites were sold on Tuesday?

3. What was the greatest number of kites sold
in one day?

4. What was the least number of kites sold
in one day?

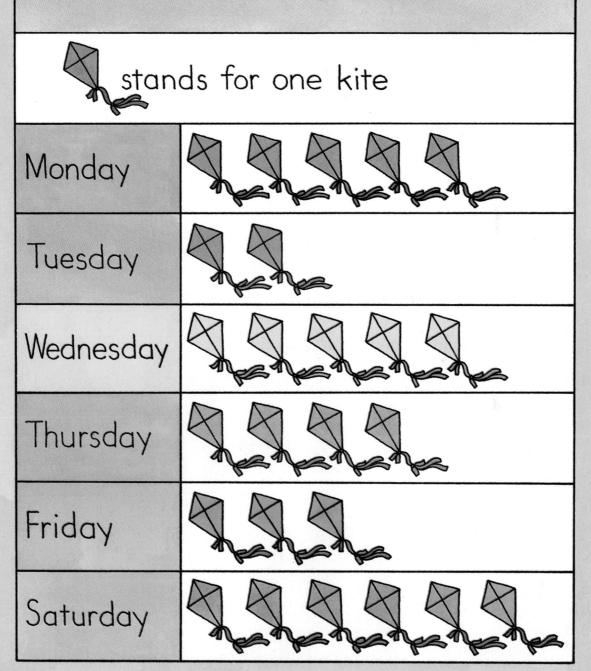

Kites Sold in One Week

🪁 stands for one kite

Monday	🪁🪁🪁🪁🪁
Tuesday	🪁🪁
Wednesday	🪁🪁🪁🪁🪁
Thursday	🪁🪁🪁🪁
Friday	🪁🪁🪁
Saturday	🪁🪁🪁🪁🪁🪁

Unit 4 Review

Main Ideas

1. All people need food, clothes, and shelter.

2. All people need love and friends.

3. Wants are things people would like to have but can live without.

4. Income is the money people earn for the work they do.

5. A service is a kind of work that people do for other people.

6. Products are things that people grow or make.

Vocabulary Review

Number your paper from **1** to **5**. Write the word that matches each picture.

product

service

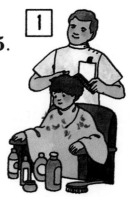

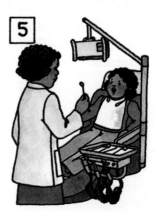

Unit Checkup

1. What are needs?
2. What three needs do all people have?
3. What are wants?
4. Why do people earn income?
5. How does a budget help people?
6. Name two service workers in your school.
7. Name three things in your home
that are goods.

Applying Knowledge

1. Make a puppet of a service worker in your community.
Draw the puppet. Color the puppet.
Cut out the puppet. Paste it on a stick.
Tell how the service worker helps your community.
2. Think of a service in your community
that is paid for with money from taxes.
Draw a picture of that service.
3. Make a list of goods that you use every day.
Share your list with a friend.

Learning About Rules and Laws

law	leader	mayor	elect
governor	capital city	President	Congress

How do rules help us?

We follow rules every day.
Rules help us in many ways.
There are rules that help us
get along with one another.
Rules about taking turns
remind us to be fair.
These kinds of rules help
give everyone a chance.

Think of rules we follow in our classroom. These rules make it easier for everyone to learn. They help make our school a pleasant place.

There are rules that protect us. These rules are called safety rules. We follow safety rules when we cross a street. Safety rules are important, too, when riding in a car. A seat belt can protect us from being injured.

What are laws?

Sometimes rules become **laws**.
Laws are rules that everyone must obey.
There are laws that help protect the rights of people.
Some laws help protect property.

All communities have laws.
Some of the laws of a community are shown on signs.
Signs remind people to obey the laws of the community.
Laws help make the community a better place
for everyone.

Who makes the laws for a community?

Every community has **leaders**.
The leaders listen to the people in the community.
They try to solve community problems.
They help make plans and laws for the community.

Most communities have a **mayor**.

The mayor is the chief leader in the community.

The mayor works with the other leaders.

The mayor helps the community make and keep its laws.

People in a community **elect,** or choose, their leaders. The people choose their leaders by voting. The votes are counted to see who is elected. The people who get the most votes are elected.

Who makes the laws for a state?

Each state in the United States has a **governor**.
The governor is the leader of the state.
The people of the state elect the governor.
The governor works with other state leaders.
Together they make plans and laws
to help everyone in the state.

Each state has a **capital city**.
The governor and other state leaders work
in the capital city.

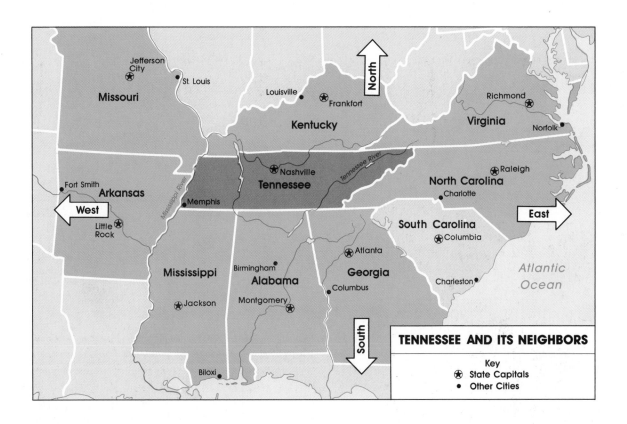

The state of Tennessee is shown on this map.
The states that are its neighbors are also shown.
The symbol for the state capital is in the key.
Nashville is the capital of Tennessee.
Find the capitals of the other states.

95

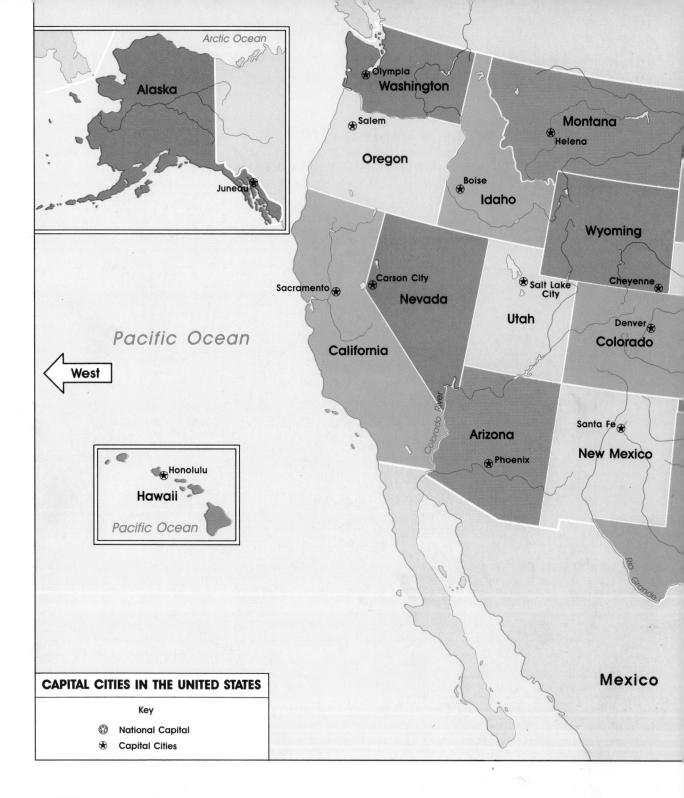

The map shows all 50 states.
It shows all 50 state capitals.

The map also shows our national capital.
Our national capital is not part of any one state.

Who makes the laws for our country?

Our country has a **President**.

The President is the leader of all the people.

The people of the United States elect the President.

The President lives and works in the White House.

The White House is in Washington, D.C.

98

The President works with **Congress**
to make plans and laws for our country.
Congress has many members.
Some are men. Some are women.
The people in each state choose leaders
to be members of Congress.

Plans and laws for the United States
are made in Washington, D.C.
Washington, D.C., is our national capital.

Comparing Drawings

Sometimes people do not like to follow rules.
Rules may not seem important.
But rules are very important.

Look at the drawings on page 101.
Find ways in which the drawings are alike.
Find ways in which they are different.

Read the questions below.
Decide which picture answers the question.
Write the numbers **1** to **4** on a sheet of paper.
Then, beside each number write the letter
of the correct picture.

1. In which drawing are people crossing
the streets safely?
2. Which drawing shows that drivers
are obeying traffic rules?
3. Which drawing shows what happens
when rules are not followed?
4. Which drawing shows that it is easier
for everyone when rules are followed?

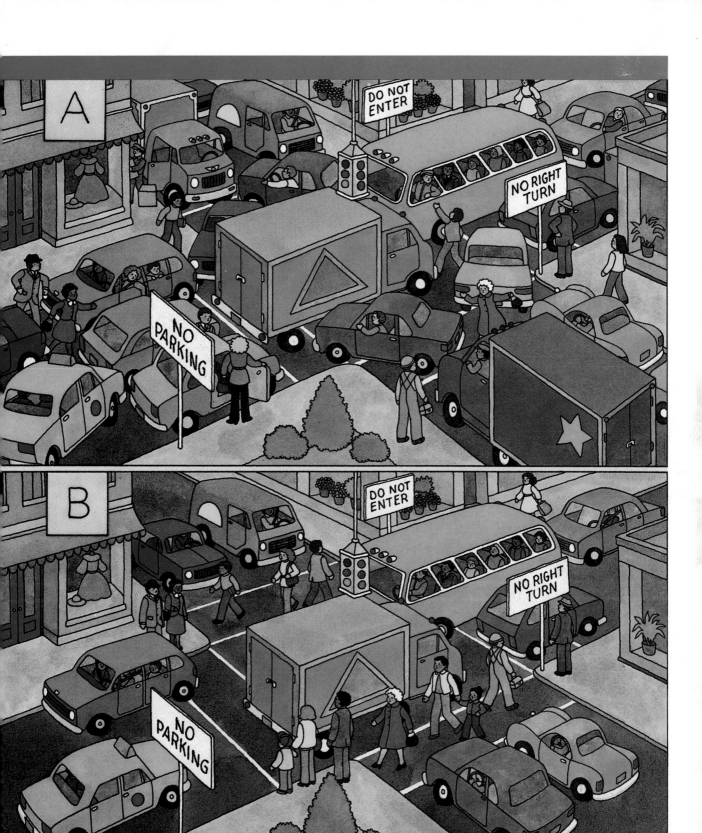

Unit 5 Review

Main Ideas

1. Rules help people get along with others.

2. Laws are rules that people must obey.

3. People elect leaders to make plans and laws.

4. The governor is the leader of the state.

5. Each state has a capital city.

6. The President is the leader of our country.

7. The President and Congress help make plans and laws for our country.

8. Washington, D.C., is the capital of our country.

Vocabulary Review

Number your paper from **1** to **6**.
Choose the right word for each sentence.

vote	governor	Congress
laws	President	capital city

1. Rules that people must obey are called ____.

2. People elect leaders when they ____.

3. The leader of the state is the ____.

4. Each state has a special city called the ____.

5. The leader of our country is the ____.

6. The President works with ____.

Unit Checkup

1. Why are rules made?
2. What are laws?
3. Why are leaders needed in the community?
4. How do people choose their leaders?
5. Who is the leader of our state?
6. Who is the leader of our country?
7. What is the name of the capital of our country?

Applying Knowledge

1. Think about a rule that helps keep people safe.
Make a poster about that rule.
Write the rule on your poster.
2. Some laws in your community are shown on signs.
Think of two signs that remind people to obey laws.
Draw a picture of each sign.

Learning About Communication and Transportation

communication

computer

transportation

subway

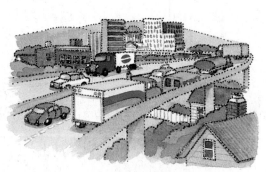
highway

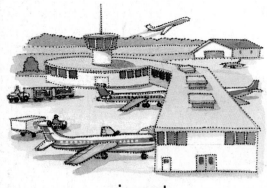
airport

port

What is communication?

How many times a day do you talk?
How often do you draw or write?
Whenever you talk, draw, or write,
you are sharing ideas.
Sharing ideas is called **communication**.

la comunidad - community
los vecinos - neighbors
los amigos - friends
la familia - famil

Whenever you laugh or cry, you show people how you feel. Laughing and crying are kinds of communication, too.

Listening to people is part of communication.
A good listener hears what someone else says.
It is important to be a good speaker.
It is also important to be a good listener.

How do we communicate?

Talking, drawing, and writing are not the only ways to communicate. Sometimes we use our hands to communicate.

Look at the pictures on this page. How are people using their hands to communicate?

What might the people be saying with their hands?

At a football game, people cheer for their team.
The sound of their cheers tells us that they are having fun.
What does the sound of a knock at a door tell us?

We can communicate through music.
Some people make beautiful sounds by singing.
Other people may play a musical instrument.
They also make beautiful music.

What are some ways we communicate today?

Long ago, people did not have many ways
to communicate.
They could talk to each other.
They could write letters.
They could communicate by using their hands.

Today we have many more ways to communicate.
We can use a telephone to talk with people.
We can listen to news or music on a radio.
We can watch our favorite shows on television.

In some schools and places of work,
people use **computers**.
A computer is a machine that helps us
communicate.
Have you ever used a computer?

What is transportation?

How many times a day do you move
from place to place?
The movement of people and products from
one place to another is called **transportation**.

Long ago, people walked
from place to place.
Later they used animals
to help them carry products.
Then people began to use
wagons on land.
Ships moved people
and products on water.
The first ships used wind
to move them.

Many years later, people rode on trains.
Trains also moved products from one place
to another.

Then cars were invented.
People and products could travel faster
and farther.
Transportation was made much easier.

How are people and products moved today?

Today people use many different kinds
of transportation.
You may come to school on a school bus.
People travel by car or truck.

In some communities people ride on **subways**.
A subway is a train that runs under the ground.

Long, wide roads, called **highways**, connect
most parts of the United States.

There are many airports in our country.
An **airport** is a place where planes land
and take off.

Ships are still used to move
people and products.
Ships load and unload
their products at special places.
These places are called **ports**.

Look at the transportation map
on pages 116 and 117.
The map shows railroads and airports.

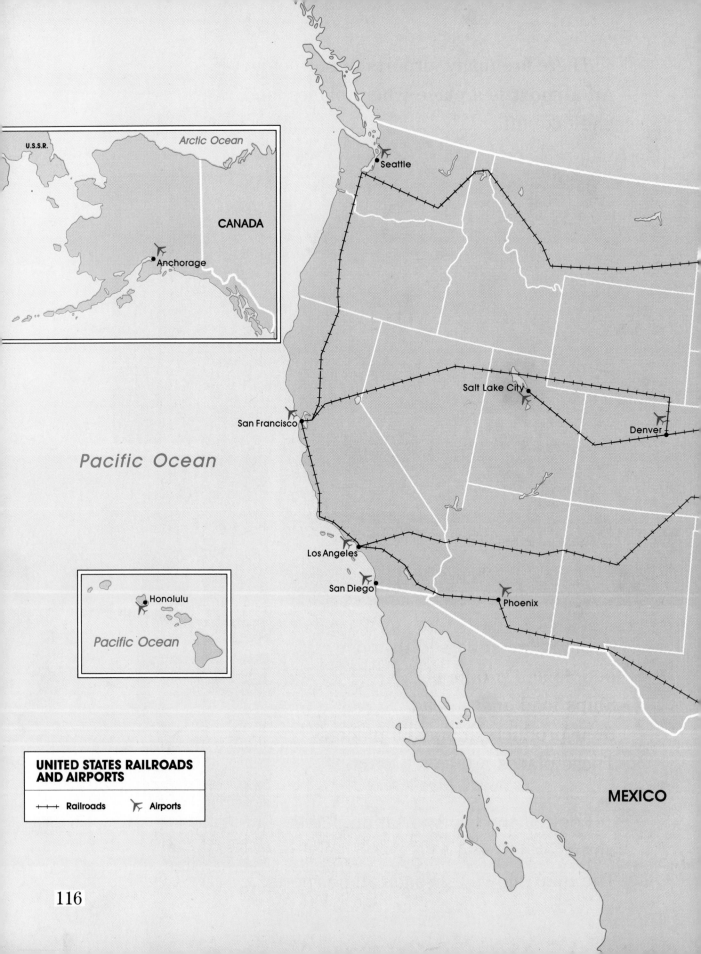

UNITED STATES RAILROADS AND AIRPORTS

Railroads   Airports

Arctic Ocean

U.S.S.R.

CANADA

Anchorage

Pacific Ocean

Seattle

Salt Lake City

Denver

San Francisco

Los Angeles

San Diego

Phoenix

MEXICO

Honolulu

Pacific Ocean

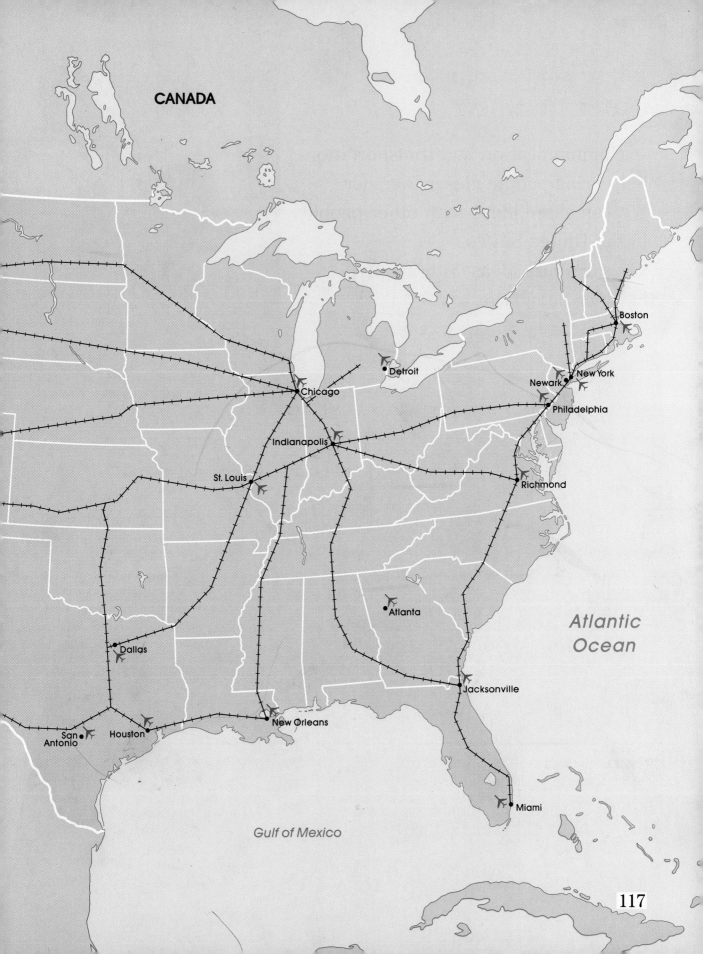

CANADA

Detroit

Chicago

Indianapolis

St. Louis

Dallas

San
Antonio

Houston

New Orleans

Atlanta

Jacksonville

Miami

Boston

New York

Newark

Philadelphia

Richmond

Atlantic
Ocean

Gulf of Mexico

What helps bring people closer together?

Communication and transportation help bring people closer together. We can share ideas with other people in the United States. We can share ideas with people in other countries. We can travel to faraway places.

Someday we may be able to travel and communicate easily in outer space.

Classifying

Today people communicate in many different ways.
There are many kinds of transportation.
Some of the pictures on page 121 show kinds of communication.
Some show kinds of transportation.

Study the pictures carefully.
Then number your paper from **1** to **5**.
Write the letter of the pictures that answer each question.

1. Which pictures show transportation?

2. Which pictures show communication?

3. Which pictures show communication by printed word?

4. Which pictures show transportation on land?

5. Which pictures show transportation that cross an ocean?

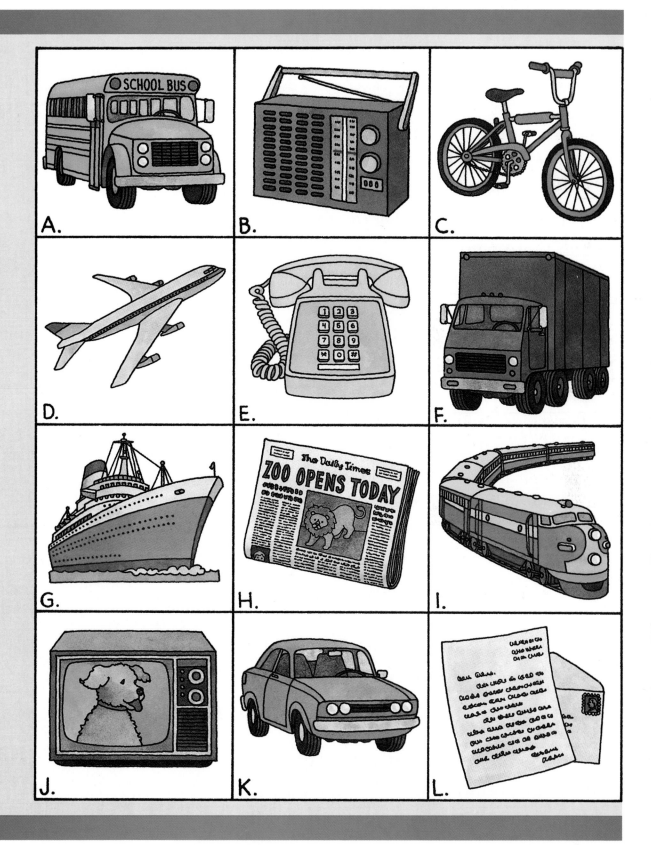

A.

B.

C.

D.

E.

F.

G.

H.

I.

J.

K.

L.

Unit 6 Review

Main Ideas

1. We communicate when we share ideas
with other people.
2. People communicate in many different ways.
3. There are more ways to communicate today
than there were long ago.
4. Transportation is moving people and
products from one place to another.
5. Communication and transportation help
bring people closer together.

Vocabulary Review

Number your paper from **1** to **5**.
Read the following sentences.
Write **T** if the sentence is true.
Write **F** if the sentence is false.

1. Listening is a part of communication.
2. A highway is a long, wide road.
3. A subway is a machine that helps people
communicate.
4. Ports are roads that connect cities.
5. Transportation helps to move people
and products from one place to another.

Unit Checkup

1. What is communication?

2. What are some ways of communicating that people have today?

3. What is transportation?

4. What are some ways of moving products today?

5. How do communication and transportation bring people closer together?

Applying Knowledge

1. Think of a sound you like to hear.
Write a story about that sound.
Tell why you like to hear the sound.

2. Find pictures showing ways people communicate today. Share the pictures with your class.

3. Draw a picture showing kinds of transportation in your community.

Learning About the First Americans

tribe

dugout canoe

longhouse

buffalo

herd

tepee

Who were the first Americans?

Long ago our country had fewer people than it has today.
The first people to live in our country were Indians.
These first Americans lived in many different places.
They lived in special groups called **tribes**.

Not all tribes were the same.
Some tribes were small. Some were large.
They lived in different kinds of homes.
They spoke different languages.

In one way the Indians were alike.
They loved the land on which they lived.
They knew how to use the land wisely.

Who were the Anasazi?

The Anasazi Indians lived
in our country a long time ago.
They lived in what today
is the state of Colorado.

The Anasazi built homes
into the sides of high steep rocks.
These rocks are called cliffs.
The Anasazi cut large stones
into blocks to build their homes.

The Anasazi were good farmers.
They grew corn, squash, and beans.
Corn, squash, and beans are crops.
Crops are plants that people grow.

Anasazi children did not go to school.
There were no schools at that time.
Children learned from members
of their family and from
older people in their tribe.
They watched and listened
and asked questions.

Who were the Makah?

Another tribe of Indians was the Makah.
They lived in what today is the state of Washington.
Find Washington on the map on pages 34 and 35.

The Makah lived near the Pacific Ocean.

There were many large trees
where the Makah lived.
They used the trees to build their homes.

Their homes were quite dark inside.
They had no windows.
At the front there was a large
carved post.
The post was called a totem pole.
A hole was cut in the totem pole
for a doorway.

Fishing was important to the Makah Indians.
They fished in rivers and in the Pacific Ocean.
They used spears and nets to catch fish.
The Makah often caught salmon.
Salmon is a special kind of fish.

The Makah built **dugout canoes** for fishing.
They hollowed out the trunks of trees
to make the canoes.
The canoes were then painted and decorated
with animal symbols.

The canoes were especially strong.
They were good for travel in deep ocean waters.

133

How did the Mohawk live?

The Mohawk Indians lived in what
today is the state of New York.
They lived in **longhouses**.
They used small trees and the bark of trees
to build their longhouses.

More than one family lived in a longhouse.
Each family had a part of the longhouse.
All the families were related to each other.

There were many rivers and lakes
where the Mohawk lived.
Canoes were used to travel by water.
The Mohawk made their canoes
from trees and bark.
Sometimes they used deerskins
instead of bark.

Mohawk men and boys hunted
and fished for food.
They hunted bear, deer, and other animals.
They used bows and arrows for hunting.

Mohawk women and girls
farmed.
They grew corn, beans, squash,
and pumpkins.
Some of the food was eaten
when it was picked.
Some of it was dried and stored away.
That food could be eaten
during the winter.

Mohawk women chose the men
to lead their tribe.
They made sure the men were good leaders.
If the men were not good leaders,
the women chose other leaders.

How did the Sioux use the buffalo?

Sioux Indians lived where three states are today.
The states are Minnesota, North Dakota,
and South Dakota.
There were many large animals
called **buffalo** in those states.

The Sioux were great hunters. They hunted buffalo
on horseback with bows and arrows.

Sometimes they hunted on foot.
They would pretend that they were wolves.
Buffalo were not afraid of wolves.

Large groups of buffalo
were called **herds**.
The Sioux moved from place
to place in search of them.

139

Each Sioux family
lived in a tent.
The tent was called
a **tepee**.
Sioux women made
the tepees.

A tepee was made by putting
buffalo skins around wooden poles.
A tepee could be easily moved.

140

The Sioux used buffalo skins
in other ways.
Buffalo skins made good blankets.
Moccasins and clothes
were made from buffalo skins.

The Sioux used every part of the buffalo.
They ate buffalo meat.
They made spoons out of buffalo horns.
Even a cradle could be made from buffalo parts.

Reading a Chart

   You have learned that the first Americans
live in groups.
Most people live in groups today.
They belong to a family, a neighborhood,
and a community.
Often, people join groups to do special things.

   Look at the chart on page 143.
It shows some groups that six children belong to.
Use the chart to answer the questions.
Write your answers on a separate sheet of paper.
Number your paper from **1** to **6**.

1. To how many groups does Amy belong?
2. To how many groups does Beth belong?
3. To how many groups does Paco belong?
4. How many children belong to the Cub Scouts?
5. Which group has the most members?
6. Which two groups have the same number
of members?

Groups We Belong To

	Brownies	Cub Scouts	Team	Reading
Amy	X			X
Beth	X		X	X
Cobb		X	X	X
Kim	X			X
Lee		X		X
Paco			X	X

Unit 7 Review

Main Ideas

1. The first people to live in our country were the Indians.

2. The Anasazi Indians once lived in what today is the state of Colorado.

3. Fishing was important to the Makah Indians.

4. Mohawk men hunted and fished for food. Mohawk women farmed.

5. The Sioux Indians hunted buffalo.

Vocabulary Review

Number your paper from **1** to **6**. Choose the right word for each sentence.

tribes	tepee	longhouse
herds	crops	dugout canoes

1. A ⎯⎯ was a home made for several families.

2. A ⎯⎯ was a home made from buffalo skins.

3. The first Americans lived in groups called ⎯⎯.

4. Corn, squash, and beans are ⎯⎯.

5. The Makah Indians used ⎯⎯ to help them fish.

6. At one time there were large ⎯⎯ of buffalo in our country.

144

Unit Checkup

1. Who were the first Americans?

2. Where did the Anasazi Indians live?

3. Near what ocean did the Makah Indians live?

4. How did the Mohawk women help their community?

5. Why were the Sioux great hunters?

Applying Knowledge

1. Draw a picture of an Indian tribe.
Put the correct kind of home in your drawing.
Add something special about the tribe.

2. Choose a tribe of Indians you have learned
about. Pretend you were a member of that
tribe. Write a story about your life.

Learning About Our Country's History

settlement

settlers

fort

wilderness

celebrate

custom

Who started the first settlement in our country?

For many years, Indians were the only people in our country.
Then other people began to come to America.
Some of these people started **settlements**.
A settlement is a small community.

People from Spain started the first settlement in the United States.
These Spanish **settlers** landed in what today is the state of Florida.
They named their settlement St. Augustine.

148

The Spanish settlers built a **fort** at St. Augustine.
A fort is a strong building or place.
They built their fort out of wood.
The fort helped to protect the Spanish
in their new land.

The Spanish settlers looked for gold in Florida.
But they found no gold there.
Some of the settlers left St. Augustine.
Other settlers did not give up.
The fort at St. Augustine was made stronger.
Slowly the settlement began to grow.

The fort still stands in St. Augustine.
It is more than 300 years old.

Today many people
visit St. Augustine.
It is the oldest city
in the United States.
Many people visit
the school.
It is the oldest wooden schoolhouse
in the United States.

People visit the blacksmith's shop.
He shows how people used to make tools.

Who started a settlement at Jamestown?

People from Spain were not the only group
to settle in America.
People came from other countries, too.
One group of people left their homes in England.
They crossed the Atlantic Ocean in three ships.
Their trip took 4 long months.

These English settlers landed in what is now
the state of Virginia.
They looked for a good place to live.
They came to a big river.
They named the river the James River
in honor of their king.
They decided to settle near the James River.
They named their settlement Jamestown.

Like the Spanish settlers, the English settlers
built a fort.
They cut down tall trees to build their fort.
Inside the fort they built houses and a church.
There also was a building where food could be stored.
They called their fort James Fort.

It was hard to get the Jamestown settlement
started.
The English settlers needed a good leader.
John Smith became their leader.

Within 2 years James Fort was crowded.
Then the settlers cleared some land beyond the fort.
They began to build houses there, too.
The place where the English settlers had landed
was no longer a **wilderness**.

We still can visit Jamestown today.
It is the oldest English settlement in our country.

When did our country become the United States of America?

Other English settlements were made
in our country after Jamestown.
The king of England ruled all these settlements.
He made laws for the people to follow.
For a long time people followed the king's laws.
Then many people began to talk about being free.
They wanted to rule themselves.

Leaders in America met to decide what to do.
They said that America should be independent.
An independent country makes its own laws.
It does not belong to any other country.

July 4, 1776 was the day the leaders decided
that America should be independent.
On that day our country became the United States
of America.
The Fourth of July is often called Independence Day.

Each year on the Fourth of July we **celebrate**
the birthday of our country.
There are parades and fireworks and picnics.
The Fourth of July reminds us that we live
in a free country.

What makes the United States a great country?

Once only part of our country was settled.
The settlers lived near the Atlantic Ocean.
Then more people began to come
to the United States.
People from all over the world came to our country.
Even today, people come to our country
from other lands.

Many people brought their own **customs**.
A custom is the special way a group of people
does something.
Some people have a special way to dance.
That is their custom.

Some people have a special way to worship.
That is their custom, too.

159

Today many people live in
the United States.
We are all Americans.
We all help to make the United States
a great country.

The United States is great because its people
are great.
We are proud to be Americans.

Putting Events in Order

Long ago what is now the United States
was a large wilderness.
Then people began to come to our country.
They made settlements. Our country grew.
Today there are many, many people in our country.

The pictures on page 163 tell part of the story
of our country.
Decide the order in which the pictures belong.
Start with what happened first in our country.
Write the letter of that picture on a sheet of paper.
Continue until you have the four pictures in order.

Unit 8 Review

Main Ideas

1. St. Augustine was the first Spanish settlement in the United States.

2. St. Augustine is the oldest city in our country.

3. Jamestown was the first English settlement in the United States.

4. On July 4, 1776, our country became the United States of America.

5. All Americans help to make the United States a great country.

Vocabulary Review

Number your paper from **1** to **5**. Write the word that completes each sentence.

fort   custom   settlement
settlers   wilderness

1. Our country was once a large _____.

2. The people who came to Jamestown were _____.

3. A strong building that protects people is a _____.

4. St. Augustine was a Spanish _____.

5. The way a group of people does something is their _____.

Unit Checkup

1. Where was the first Spanish settlement in our country started?

2. Why do many people visit St. Augustine today?

3. Why do we remember the settlement at Jamestown?

4. How did John Smith help the Jamestown settlers?

5. When do we celebrate the birthday of our country?

Applying Knowledge

1. Imagine that you lived in the Jamestown settlement.
Think of games that you might have played.
Draw a picture of yourself playing with friends.

2. Bring to class pictures that show
your community long ago.
Maybe your family can help you.
See if anyone knows what the places look like now.

Learning About Holidays

holiday

Pilgrims

feast

pioneers

monument

veteran

Why do we remember Christopher Columbus?

Christopher Columbus lived a long time ago.
He lived in a country called Spain.
Columbus sailed across the Atlantic Ocean
to America.
His ship was called the Santa Maria.
Two other ships followed him.
One was named the Niña.
The other was the Pinta.

We still remember Christopher Columbus.
We have a **holiday** in October to honor him.
It is called Columbus Day.
We celebrate Columbus Day on the second Monday
in October.
On that day we remember that Columbus landed
in America.

Why is Thanksgiving Day a special day?

The **Pilgrims** were a group of people
who came to America a long time ago.
They landed in Plymouth. Plymouth is
in what today is the state of Massachusetts.

Friendly Indians helped the Pilgrims.
They showed the Pilgrims how to hunt and fish.
They showed them where to grow food.

The Pilgrims were thankful for their new life.
They decided to have a **feast** to celebrate.
They invited all their Indian friends.
The Pilgrims thanked God for their food.
They thanked God for the Indians.
This was the first Thanksgiving.

Each year we celebrate Thanksgiving Day
on the fourth Thursday in November.
Our families come together.
We give thanks for everything we have.

Who was Martin Luther King, Jr.?

Martin Luther King, Jr., had a dream for our country.
He wanted all people to be treated fairly.
He asked people to care about other people.

King worked hard to make his dream come true.
He became a leader in our country.
He led people who wanted a better life
for all black people.

King often spoke to large
crowds of people.

Today all Americans remember
Martin Luther King, Jr.
We honor him on the third
Monday in January.

Who was Abraham Lincoln?

Abraham Lincoln was a
great American.
He was born in Kentucky
on February 12, 1809.
His family were **pioneers**.
A pioneer is a person who
leads the way to a new land.
The Lincoln family moved
to Indiana.
Later they moved to Illinois.
This picture shows their home
in Illinois.

Pioneer life was hard.
Pioneer children did not have
much time for school.
Lincoln liked to read
when he was a boy.
He taught himself many things.

Lincoln became the sixteenth
President of the United States.
He was a friend to all people.
We celebrate Lincoln's
birthday in February.

A beautiful **monument** was
built to honor Abraham Lincoln.
It is in Washington, D.C.

Why do we remember George Washington?

England once ruled our country.
Many Americans did not want to be ruled by England.
They wanted to be free.
They decided to win their freedom from England.
They asked George Washington to lead them.

Washington led the Americans against England.
The struggle was long and hard.
At last the Americans became free.

176

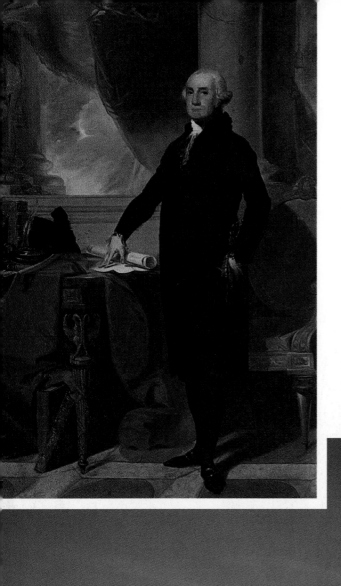

The people of our country
admired George Washington.
They wanted him
to continue to lead them.
They made him the first
President of the United States.
Washington helped our country
become a strong nation.
We celebrate his birthday on
the third Monday in February.

What is Arbor Day?

Trees help make our country beautiful.
Trees are useful, too.
They shade houses from the sun.
They give us many good things to eat.
Fruits and nuts come from trees.

In our country there is a special day for
planting trees.
It is called Arbor Day.
Arbor Day comes when the weather is good for planting.

Many school children plant a tree on Arbor Day.
Then, all year long, they take care of their tree.

What is Memorial Day?

The United States of America is a free country.
Many people have helped keep our country free.
Some of these people died to keep our country free.
We are proud of all those people.
We have a special day to honor them.
It is called Memorial Day.

On Memorial Day there are parades in almost every community.
Often **veterans** march in the parade.
A veteran is a person who has served in the armed forces.
Groups of school children usually march in the parade, too.

On Memorial Day we also remember family and friends who are no longer living.
Memorial Day is celebrated in May.

When do we celebrate Flag Day?

The American flag is a symbol of our country.
It stands for our country.
Our first flag had 13 stars and 13 stripes.
When our country became free, there were
13 states.
A star and a stripe was put in the flag for each state.

Today our flag still has 13 stripes
to honor our first 13 states.
But now there are 50 stars in the flag.
Each star stands for one of our 50 states.

Each year on June 14
we celebrate Flag Day.
Flag Day reminds us
that our flag is special.

Reading a Time Line

We celebrate holidays throughout the year.
Some holidays come at the beginning of the year.
Some come in the middle of the year.
Some come near the end of the year.

There is a special kind of drawing below.
It is called a time line.
A time line shows the order in which things happen.

Lincoln's Birthday

Washington's Birthday

Memorial Day

Martin Luther King, Jr.,
Day

| January | February | March | April | May | June |

Study the time line. Then answer these questions.
Write your answers on a separate sheet of paper.

1. Which holiday is in January?
2. How many holidays are there in February?
3. Which holiday is in July?
4. Which holiday is in November?
5. Which holiday follows Washington's Birthday?
6. Which holiday is between Independence Day
and Thanksgiving Day?

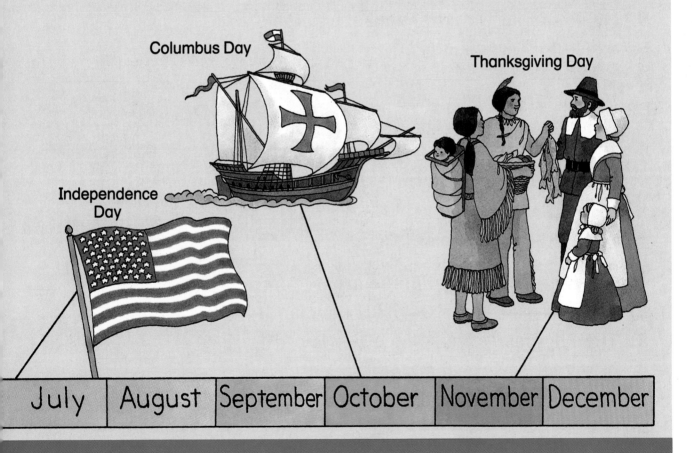

Columbus Day

Thanksgiving Day

Independence
Day

| July | August | September | October | November | December |

Unit 9 Review

Main Ideas

1. Christopher Columbus sailed to America.

2. On Thanksgiving Day we give thanks
for everything we have.

3. Martin Luther King, Jr., wanted all people
to be treated fairly.

4. Abraham Lincoln was the sixteenth President
of the United States.

5. George Washington was the first President
of the United States.

6. On Memorial Day we honor the people
who died for our country.

Vocabulary Review

Number your paper form **1** to **5**.
Write T if the sentence is true.
Write F if the sentence is false.

1. A veteran has served in the armed forces.

2. A pioneer leads the way to a new land.

3. The Pilgrims started Memorial Day.

4. A holiday is a special kind of meal.

5. The Lincoln Memorial is a monument.

Unit Checkup

1. When do we celebrate Columbus Day?

2. How did the Pilgrims celebrate Thanksgiving?

3. What dream did Martin Luther King, Jr., have for the United States?

4. Who was Abraham Lincoln?

5. How did George Washington help our country?

6. Whom do we honor on Memorial Day?

Applying Knowledge

1. Pretend that you were at the first Thanksgiving. Make a list of what you would be thankful for.

2. Choose the holiday you like best. Make a greeting card for that holiday. Draw a picture of your greeting card. Write a message on your greeting card.

Atlas

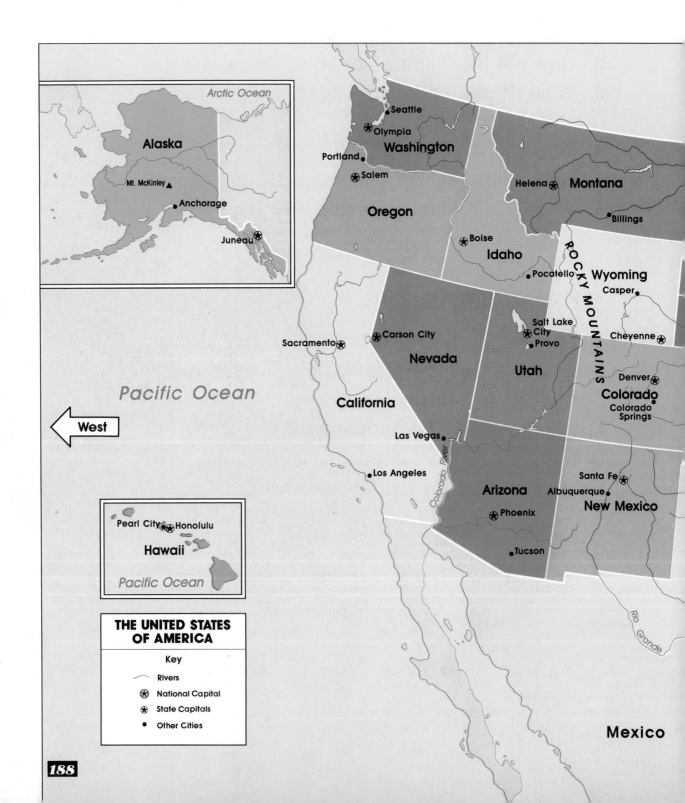

Arctic Ocean

Alaska

Mt. McKinley ▲

● Anchorage

Juneau ⊛

● Seattle
⊛ Olympia
Washington
Portland ●
⊛ Salem
Oregon

Helena ⊛ Montana
● Billings
⊛ Boise
Idaho
● Pocatello Wyoming
Casper ●

Pacific Ocean

Sacramento ⊛
Carson City ●
Nevada

Salt Lake ● City
● Provo
Utah

ROCKY MOUNTAINS

Cheyenne ⊛

Denver ⊛
Colorado
Colorado Springs ●

West

California

Las Vegas ●

Colorado River

● Los Angeles

Arizona

Santa Fe ⊛
Albuquerque ●
New Mexico

⊛ Phoenix

● Tucson

Pearl City ● ⊛ Honolulu
Hawaii
Pacific Ocean

Rio Grande

Mexico

THE UNITED STATES
OF AMERICA

Key

⌒ Rivers
⊛ National Capital
⊛ State Capitals
● Other Cities

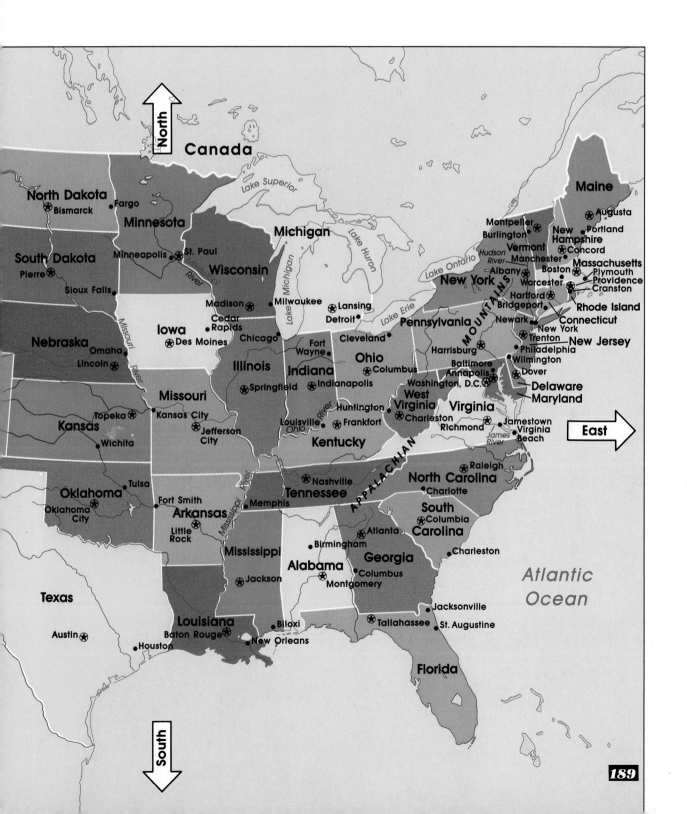

North

Canada

Lake Superior

North Dakota
● Bismarck
● Fargo

Minnesota

Lake Huron

Michigan

Maine

⊛ Augusta

Montpelier
Burlington ● ⊛ New
Vermont Hampshire ● Portland
Manchester ● ⊛ Concord

South Dakota
● Pierre ⊛

Minneapolis ⊛
● St. Paul
Wisconsin

Lake Michigan

Hudson
River
Albany ⊛
● Boston
Massachusetts
● Plymouth
Providence
● Cranston

Sioux Falls ●

Madison ⊛
● Milwaukee

⊛ Lansing
Detroit ●

New York

Lake Ontario

Worcester ●
Hartford ⊛
Bridgeport ●

Rhode Island

Missouri River

Iowa

Cedar ●
Rapids

Chicago ●

Lake Erie

Cleveland ●

Pennsylvania

MOUNTAINS

Connecticut

Newark ●
● New York

Nebraska
● Omaha
● Lincoln

⊛ Des Moines

Fort ●
Wayne

Ohio

⊛ Columbus

Harrisburg ⊛

Baltimore ●
Annapolis ⊛

● Trenton
● Philadelphia
● Wilmington

New Jersey

Illinois

Indiana

Springfield ⊛
● Indianapolis

● Dover

Delaware
Maryland

Missouri

Topeka ⊛
Kansas
● Wichita

● Kansas City

⊛ Jefferson
City

Louisville ●
Ohio River

Huntington ●
● Frankfort

West
Virginia
● Charleston

Washington, D.C. ⊛

Virginia

Richmond ●

Jamestown
● Virginia
Beach
James
River

East

Kentucky

Oklahoma
Oklahoma ⊛
City

● Tulsa

Fort Smith ●

Mississippi River

⊛ Nashville

Tennessee

APPALACHIAN

Raleigh ●
North Carolina
● Charlotte

Arkansas

● Memphis

Little ●
Rock

Mississippi

⊛ Jackson

● Biloxi

Alabama

Birmingham ●

● Columbus
Montgomery ●

South
⊛ Columbia
Carolina

Georgia

● Charleston

Texas

Atlanta ⊛

Jacksonville ●

Austin ⊛

Louisiana
Baton Rouge ⊛

● New Orleans

● Houston

⊛ Tallahassee ● St. Augustine

Florida

Atlantic
Ocean

South

189

Arctic Ocean

Greenland
(Denmark)

Union of Soviet
Socialist Republics

Alaska
(United States)

Canada

Great
Lakes

United States of America

Atlantic Ocean

Mexico

Hawaii (United States)

Cuba

Puerto Rico
(United States)

Guatemala

Honduras

El Salvador

Nicaragua

Caribbean
Sea

Costa Rica

Pacific Ocean

Panama

Venezuela

Colombia

Ecuador

West

Peru

Brazil

Bolivia

Paraguay

New Zealand

Chile

Uruguay

Argentina

THE WORLD

190

South

North

Arctic Ocean

Iceland

Norway
Sweden Finland

Union of Soviet Socialist Republics

Denmark
Ireland United Kingdom
Poland
Czechoslovakia
France
Yugoslavia
Italy
Bulgaria
Portugal Spain
Mediterranean Sea
Greece
Turkey
Morocco
Tunisia
Syria
Iraq
Jordan
Iran
Afghanistan
Pakistan

China

North Korea
South Korea
Japan

Algeria
Libya
Egypt
Qatar
Saudi Arabia

Mauritania
Mali
Niger
Chad
Sudan

Bangladesh
India
Burma
Laos
Thailand Vietnam
Taiwan

Senegal
Gambia
Guinea
Sierra Leone
Liberia
Ghana
Ivory Coast
Nigeria
Cameroon
Ethiopia
Somalia
Kenya

Sri Lanka

Philippines

East

Gabon
Zaire
Tanzania

Malaysia

Indonesia

Angola
Zambia Malawi
Mozambique
Zimbabwe
Madagascar

Indian Ocean

Atlantic Ocean

South Africa

Australia

Place Geography Dictionary

You can find each place on a map in your book. The pages tell you where the maps are.

Africa
One of the earth's seven continents. Pages 46–47

Australia
The earth's smallest continent. Pages 46–47

Alaska
The largest state in size in the United States. Pages 34–35

California
The state with the most people. Pages 34–35

Antarctica
One of the earth's seven continents. Pages 46–47

Canada
The country that is directly north of the United States. Page 45

Arctic Ocean
The largest body of salt water near the North Pole. Pages 46–47

Colorado
A state in the western part of the United States. Pages 34–35

Asia
The earth's largest continent. Pages 46–47

Columbus
A city in Ohio. Page 33

Atlantic Ocean
The largest body of salt water along the eastern coast of the United States. Pages 46–47

England
Part of the country of Great Britain from which the Pilgrims came. Pages 190–191

Europe

The earth's second smallest continent. Pages 46–47

Indian Ocean

A body of salt water between Africa and Asia. Pages 46–47

Florida

A state in the southern part of the United States that is part of a peninsula. Pages 34–35

James River

A river in Virginia. Jamestown was settled along the James River. Pages 188–189

Hawaii

A state in the United States made up entirely of islands. Pages 34–35

Jamestown

The oldest English settlement in America. It is located on the James River. Pages 188–189

Hudson River

A river that flows through New York state into the Atlantic Ocean. Pages 188–189

Kentucky

A state that borders on seven states. Pages 34–35

Illinois

A state that borders on Lake Michigan. Pages 34–35

Massachusetts

A state that borders on the Atlantic Ocean. Pages 34–35

Indiana

A state that borders on Lake Michigan. Pages 34–35

Mexico

The country that is directly south of the United States. Page 45

Minnesota

A state that borders on Canada and Lake Superior. Pages 34–35

North Dakota

A state that borders on Canada. Pages 34–35

Mount McKinley

Located in Alaska. It is the highest mountain peak in North America. Pages 188–189

Ohio

A state the borders on Lake Erie. Page 33

Nashville

The capital city of Tennessee. Page 95

Oklahoma

A state that borders on six states. Pages 34–35

New York

A state that borders on Lake Ontario, Lake Erie, and the Atlantic Ocean. Pages 34–35

Pacific Ocean

The earth's largest body of salt water. It is off the west coast of the United States. Pages 46–47

North America

The earth's third largest continent. Page 45

Plymouth

The second oldest English settlment in America. Plymouth is in Massachusetts. Pages 188–189

North Carolina

A state in the southern part of the United States that borders on the Atlantic Ocean. Pages 34–35

St. Augustine

A city in Florida. It is the oldest city in the United States. Pages 188–189

South America

The earth's fourth largest continent.
Pages 46–47

South Dakota

A state that borders on six states.
Pages 34–35

Spain

A country on the continent of Europe.
Pages 190–191

Tennessee

A state that borders on eight states.
Page 95

United States of America

Our country that stretches from the Atlantic Ocean to the Pacific Ocean.
Pages 34–35

Virginia

A state in the southern part of the United States.
Pages 34–35

Washington

A northern state that borders on the Pacific Ocean. Pages 34–35

Washington, D.C.

The capital city of the United States.
Pages 96–97

PLACE GEOGRAPHY DICTIONARY

PLACE GEOGRAPHY DICTIONARY

Picture Dictionary

The page numbers tell where each word first appears in the text.

airport. A place where airplanes land and take off. p. 115.

apartment building. A building that has separate homes for many families. p. 6.

budget. A spending plan to help people decide how to use their money. p. 69.

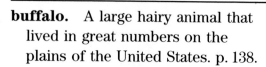

buffalo. A large hairy animal that lived in great numbers on the plains of the United States. p. 138.

capital city. The city where leaders of a country or state meet and work. p. 95.

celebrate. Do special things on a birthday or holiday. p. 157.

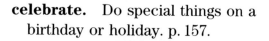

city. A large community where many people live and work. p. 6.

communication. Sharing ideas with others. p. 106.

community. People who live in a certain area or place. p. 4.

computer. A machine that does some kinds of work faster and makes some kinds of work easier. p. 111.

Congress. The men and women chosen to help make laws for all the people in our country. p. 99.

continent. One of the seven large bodies of land on the earth. Our continent is North America. p. 44.

country. A large area of land and the people who live there. The United States is our country. p. 34.

custom. The special way a group of people does something. p. 159.

direction. The way in which a person or thing faces, points, or moves. p. 29.

dugout canoe. A boat made by hollowing out a large log. p. 133.

east. The direction from which the sun seems to rise each morning. p. 30.

elect. To choose leaders by voting. p. 93.

factory. A place where products are made. p. 7.

feast. A meal prepared for a special occasion. p. 171.

fort. A strong building or place made for protection. p. 149.

globe. A small model of the earth. p. 49.

governor. A person who is elected by the people of a state to be their leader. p. 94.

herd. A group of large animals of one kind. p. 139.

highway. A main road between one town or city and another. p. 114.

holiday. A special day to remember a person or an event. p. 169.

income. The money people earn for the work they do. p. 68.

island. A body of land that has water all around it. p. 54.

key. A special part of a map that explains the symbols on the map. p. 24.

lake. A body of water with land all around it. p. 54.

law. A rule that people must obey. p. 90.

leader. A person who leads a group of people. p. 92.

longhouse. A house built by Indians in which a number of families lived. p. 134.

map. A flat drawing of the earth or part of the earth. p. 24.

mayor. The most important elected leader of a community. p. 93.

model. A small-scale copy of an object. A globe is a model of the earth. p. 49.

monument. Something set up to honor a person or an event. p. 175.

mountain. Very high land that rises above the land around it. p. 53.

museum. A building where interesting objects are collected and displayed. p. 9.

needs. Things that all people must have to live. p. 62.

neighborhood. A small part of a community in a town or city. p. 4.

north. The direction toward the North Pole. p. 30.

ocean. A large body of salt water. p. 47.

peninsula. A piece of land that has water nearly all around it. A peninsula is part of a larger body of land. p. 55.

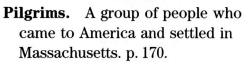

Pilgrims. A group of people who came to America and settled in Massachusetts. p. 170.

pioneer. A person who leads the way to a new land. p. 174.

plain. A level area of land. p. 52.

port. A place where ships load and unload products. p. 115.

President. The leader of our country. p. 98.

products. Things that are made and sold. Food and clothes are products. p. 74.

river. A long body of water that flows through the land. p. 53.

savings. Money saved out of income. p. 69.

services. Kinds of work other than making products. p. 70.

settler. A person who starts a community in a new country. p. 148.

settlement. A small community. p. 148.

south. The direction toward the South Pole. p. 30.

state. One of the 50 parts of the United States. p. 32.

suburb. A city or town near a large city. p. 10.

subway. A train that runs under the ground. p. 114.

symbol. A drawing or an object that stands for a real place or thing. p. 24.

House
Street
Water

taxes. Money people pay to their government. p. 73.

tepee. A cone-shaped house made by putting buffalo skins around wooden poles. p. 140.

town. A small community with few homes and stores. p. 15.

transportation. The movement of people and products from one place to another. p. 112.

tribe. A large group of people living together who share the same beliefs, such as a tribe of Indians. p. 126.

veteran. A person who has served in the armed forces. p. 181.

wants. Things that people like to have but do not need. p. 66.

west. The direction toward which the sun seems to set. p. 30.

wilderness. An area of land that has not been changed by people. p. 155.

Index

Credits

Cover: Cheryl Griffin for Silver Burdett & Ginn

Contributing artists: Ethel Gold, Tad Krumeich, Yoshi Miyake, Hubert Wackermann, David Wenzel

All photographs by Silver Burdett & Ginn unless otherwise noted.

Table of Contents iii: Unit One, Clyde H. Smith/F Stop Pictures; Unit Three, Ed Cooper/H. Armstrong Roberts. iv: Unit Five, H. Abernathy/H. Armstrong Roberts; Unit 6, Dick Patterson/Shostal Associates; Unit Seven, Manley Photo/Shostal Associates; Unit Eight, Michal Heron for Silver Burdett & Ginn. 1: Unit Nine, © Hella Hammid/Rapho/Photo Researchers, Inc.

Unit One 3: Clyde H. Smith/F Stop Pictures. 4: Peter LeGrand/Click, Chicago. 5: *t.* © David R. Frazier/Photo Researchers, Inc.; *inset* Three Lions; *b.l.* Ethan Hoffman/Archive Pictures, Inc.; *b.r.* Ken Kerbs for Silver Burdett & Ginn. 6: *t.* William R. Wright/Taurus Photos; *b.* Joan Liftin/Archive Pictures, Inc. 7: *r.* Eric Carle/Shostal Associates; *l.* courtesy of Matchbox, Lesney Products, Inc. 8: *t.* David Woo/Stock, Boston; *b.* Ann Hagen Griffiths/O.P.C. 9: *t.* © Joseph Nettis/Photo Researchers, Inc.; *b.* Walter Frerck/Odyssey Productions. 10: Randy Brandon/Aperture. 11. *m.* David Madison/Bruce Coleman; *b.* Titmus/Taurus Photos. 12: *t.* Ralph Krubner; *b.* Richard Steedman/Stock Market. 14: *t.* © Lowell J. Georgia/Photo Researchers, Inc.; *b.* Craig Aurness/West Light. 15: *t.* Paul O. Boisvert/Alpha. 16: *t.m.* Craig Aurness/Click, Chicago; *t.l.* © Peter Miller/Photo Researchers, Inc.; *b.* © Calvin Larsen/Photo Researchers, Inc. 17: *t.* © Peter Miller/Photo Researchers, Inc.; *b.* Robert Frerck/Odyssey Productions.

Unit Two 24: Cheryl Griffin. 32: © Georg Gerster/Photo Researchers, Inc.

Unit Three 43: Ed Cooper/H. Armstrong Roberts. 44: © Roy Hankey/Photo Researchers, Inc. 48: NASA. 52: *t.* © Russ Kinne/Photo Researchers, Inc. 52–53: *b.* Tony Linck/Shostal Associates. 53: Rick Mc Intyre/ Alaska Photo. 54: *b.* William Felger/Grant Heilman Photography. 55: Patrick Grace/Taurus Photos.

Unit Four 62: © Richard Hutchings/Photo Researchers, Inc. 63: *b.* © Susan Johns/Rapho/Photo Researchers, Inc. 64: Cathy Melloan/Click, Chicago. 65: *t.* © Tom McHugh/Photo Researchers, Inc. 65: *b.* Cheryl Griffin. 66: *t.* Ken Lax for Silver Burdett & Ginn, photo courtesy of Josh 'n Abby, Inc.; *b.* Bruce Waters/Uniphoto. 67: © Richard Hutchings/Photo Researchers, Inc. *b.* Donald Dietz/Stock, Boston. 68: Dan De Wilde for Silver Burdett & Ginn. 70: *t.* Don Klumpp; *b.* Bob Hahn/Taurus Photos. 71: *l.* © Van Bucher/Photo Researchers, Inc.; *r.* © Jan Halaska/Photo Researchers, Inc.; *b.* Mark Sherman/Bruce Coleman. 72: *l.* David Falconer/West Stock; *r.* © Roger Foley/Photo Researchers, Inc. 73: *t.* G. Kubica, Jr./Shostal Associates; *r.* Ann Hagen Griffiths/O.P.C. 74: © Richard Hutchings/Photo Researchers, Inc. 75: *t.l.* © Melissa Grimes-Guy/Photo Researchers, Inc.; *t.r.* © Geoff Gilbert/Photo Researchers, Inc.; *m.l.* © Edward Lettau/Photo Researchers, Inc.; *b.* © Dick Luria/Science Source/Photo Researchers, Inc. 76 *b.*–80: Ed Bock for Silver Burdett & Ginn.

Unit Five 87: H. Abernathy/H. Armstrong Roberts; 88: *t.* E.R. Degginger; *b.* © Richard Hutchings/Photo Researchers, Inc. 89: *t.* Joe Viesti for Silver Burdett & Ginn; *b.l.* L.L.T. Rhodes/Taurus Photos. 91: *r.* Cheryl Griffin. 92: © Peter Miller/Photo Researchers, Inc. 93: *t.* Joe Skymba/Berg & Associates. 94: R. Krubner/H. Armstrong Roberts. 98: © Kul Bhatia/Photo Researchers, Inc. 99: Gene Ahrens/Shostal Associates.

Unit Six 105: Dick Patterson/Shostal Associates. 106: *l.* Frank Siteman/Stock, Boston; *r.* Joe Viesti for Silver Burdett & Ginn. 107: *t.* Lenore Weber/O.P.C.; *b.* Ellis Herwig/Stock, Boston. 108: *t.* Alec Duncan/Taurus Photos; *m.* Joe Viesti for Silver Burdett & Ginn; *b.* Kenneth Karp/O.P.C. 109: *t.* Don Smetzer/Click, Chicago. 110: *t.l.* Victoria Beller-Smith/E.R. Degginger; *r.* Michal P. Manheim. 111: Brownie Harris/ Stock Market. 112: *t.* William Hamilton/Shostal Associates; *b.* Shostal Associates. 113: *t.* H. Armstrong Roberts; *inset* Fred M. Dole/F Stop Pictures. 114: *t.l.* Joe Viesti; *t.r.* Brian Smith/Stock, Boston; *b.* Thomas Braise/Stock Market. 115. *t.* Ward Wells/Shostal Associates; *b.* Norman R. Thompson/Taurus Photos. 118: *b.* © Tom McHugh/Photo Researchers, Inc. 119: © M. Paternostro/Photo Researchers, Inc.

Unit Seven 125: Manley Photo/Shostal Associates. 126: *l.* L.L.T. Rhodes/Click, Chicago; *t.m.* © Porterfield-Chickering/Photo Researchers, Inc.; *b.m.* Roy Morsch/Stock Market; *t.r.* Ray Shaw/Stock Market; *b.r.* © Nancy Wood/Photo Researchers, Inc. 127: Bob Brudd/Click, Chicago; *inset* Courtesy Department Library Services, American Museum of Natural History.

Unit Eight 147: Michal Heron for Silver Burdett & Ginn. 150–151: Kevin Kolczynski for Silver Burdett & Ginn. 157: *b.l.* Charles Krebs/Aperture. 158: The Bettmann Archive. 159: *t.* Bill Bryant/Shostal Associates; *b.l.* Ted Horowitz/Stock Market; *b.r.* © Blair Seitz/Photo Researchers, Inc. 160: *t.* Gabe Palmer/Stock Market; *b.* Cheryl Griffin. 161: Michal Heron for Silver Burdett & Ginn.

Unit Nine 167: © Hella Hammid/Rapho/Photo Researchers, Inc. 168: The Granger Collection. 169: Dan De Wilde for Silver Burdett & Ginn. 170: J.L.G. Ferres/Historical Pictures Service. 171: Norman Rockwell Museum. 172: Flip Schulke. 173: *t.* UPI/Bettmann Newsphotos; *b.* Ray C. Moore/Shostal Associates. 174: *t.* © Tom McHugh/Photo Researchers, Inc., courtesy of the National Portrait Gallery; *b.* Historical Pictures Service. 175: *t.* Culver Pictures, Inc.; *b.* © Everett Johnson/Folio, Inc. 176–177:*t.* The Granger Collection. 177: *b.* Joe Viesti for Silver Burdett & Ginn. 178: David A. Bast; *inset* Grant Heilman Photography. 180: Dennis Brack/Black Star. 181: Cheryl Griffin. 182: *t.* Bob Daemmrich; *b.* Elizabeth Crews/Stock, Boston.

B C D E F G H—RRD—97 96 95 94 93 92 91 90 89